Community Helpers

Doctors

by Dee Ready

Reading Consultant:
Dr. Charles Sneiderman, MD Ph.D.
Diplomate, American Board of Family Practice

Bridgestone Books
an Imprint of Capstone Press

Bridgestone Books are published by Capstone Press
151 Good Counsel Drive, P.O. Box 669, Mankato, Minnesota 56002
http://www.capstone-press.com

Library of Congress Cataloging-in-Publication Data
Ready, Dee.
    Doctors/by Dee Ready.
    p. cm.—(Community helpers)
    Includes bibliographical references and index.
    Summary: Explains the clothing, tools, schooling, and work of doctors.
    ISBN 1-56065-509-7
    1. Physicians—Juvenile literature. 2. Medicine—Juvenile literature.
[1. Physicians. 2. Medicine. 3. Occupations.] I. Title. II. Series: Community
helpers (Mankato, Minn.)
R690.R38   1997
610.69'52—dc21
                                                        96-47306
                                                        CIP

Photo credits
International Stock/Westerman, cover: Hal Kern, 6; Tom Carroll, 20
FPG, 12; Michael Keller, 4; Jeffrey Myers, 8; Jim McNee, 16
Unicorn/Tom McCarthy, 10; Bev Hoffmann, 14; R. Nolan, 18

Table of Contents

Doctors

Doctors help sick people get better.
They also try to stop people from
becoming sick. People go to doctors for
checkups. A checkup is an exam to see
if a person is healthy.

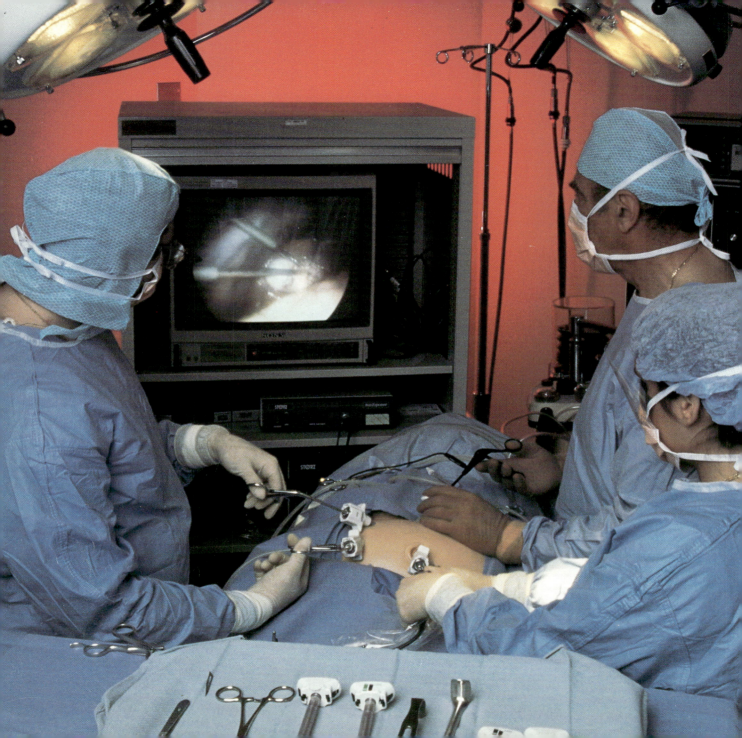

What Doctors Do

Doctors try to fix what is wrong with a sick person. Sometimes doctors need to do surgery. Surgery is cutting open part of the body to fix a problem. Doctors give patients medicine so surgery does not hurt.

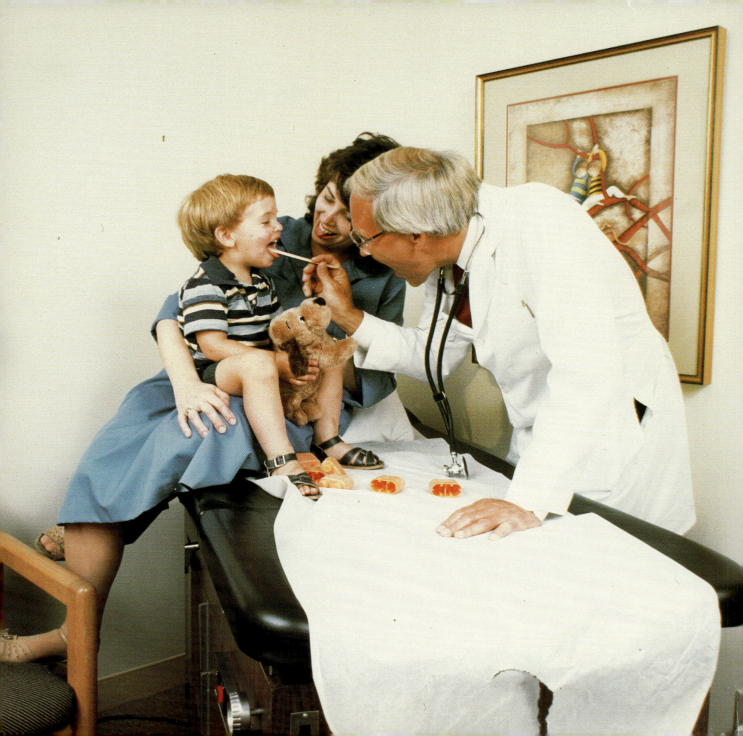

Different Kinds of Doctors

All doctors learn about the whole body. Some choose to study special parts of the body. Other doctors care for certain kinds of patients. A doctor who sees only children is called a pediatrician.

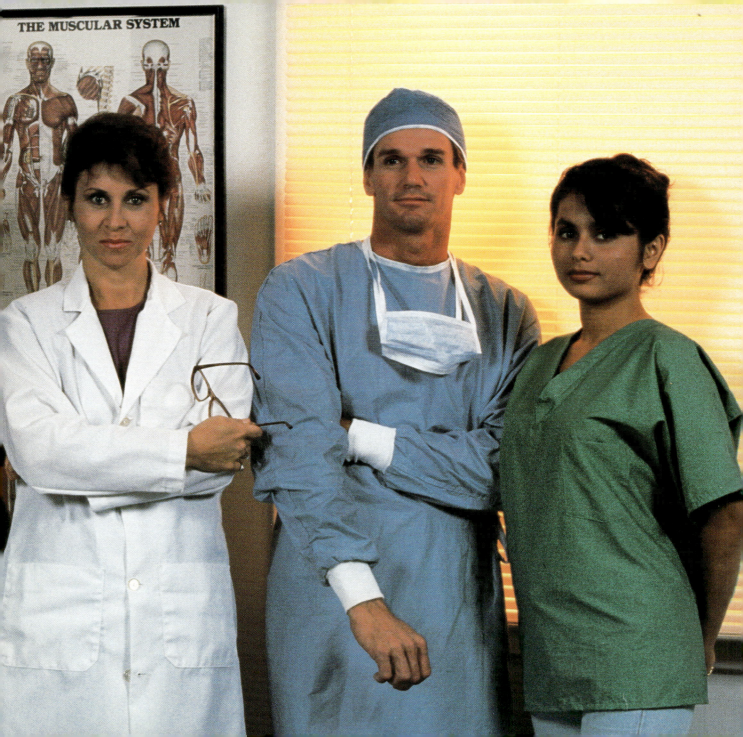

What Doctors Wear

Many doctors wear a white coat while seeing patients. Some doctors wear scrubs. Scrubs are loose-fitting shirts and pants. Doctors sometimes wear rubber gloves.

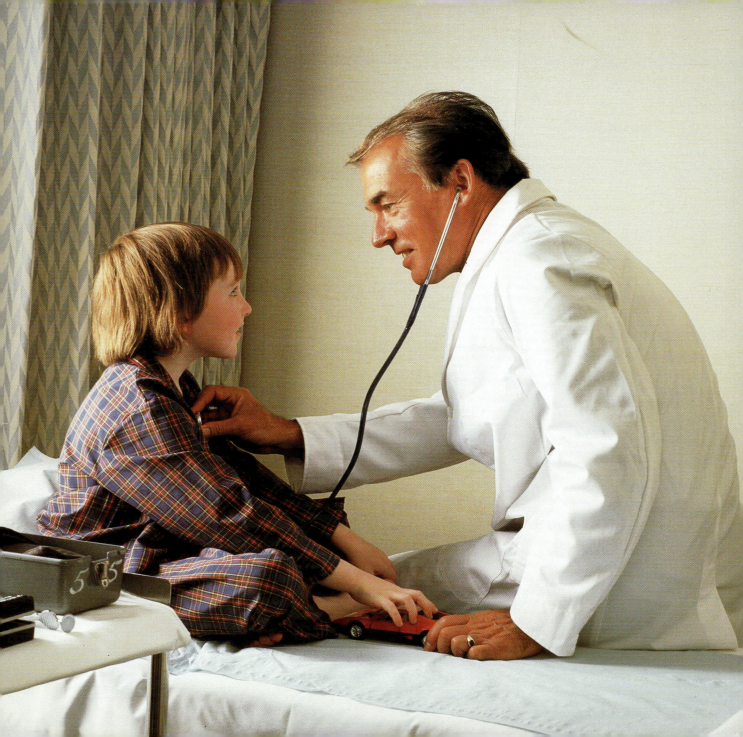

Tools Doctors Use

During a checkup, doctors use a stethoscope to listen to the sounds in a patient's chest. They check a patient's eyes and ears with special lights. Doctors sometimes use special machines to find other problems.

Doctors and School

Doctors go to college and medical school for eight years. Then they work as student doctors in hospitals for up to six years. After that, they can become specialists.

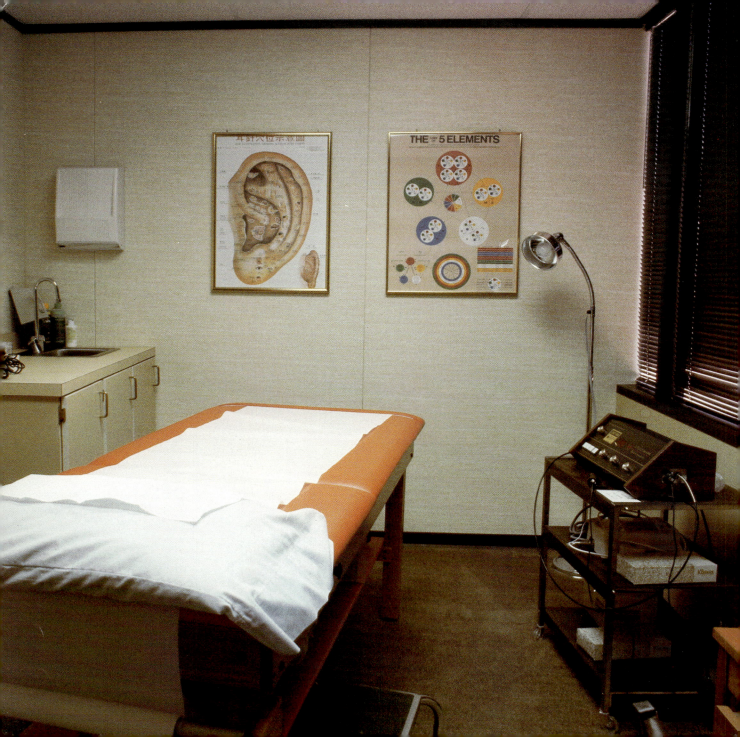

Where Doctors Work

Doctors usually work in hospitals or clinics. Some doctors run their own offices. A few doctors visit nursing homes and poor communities.

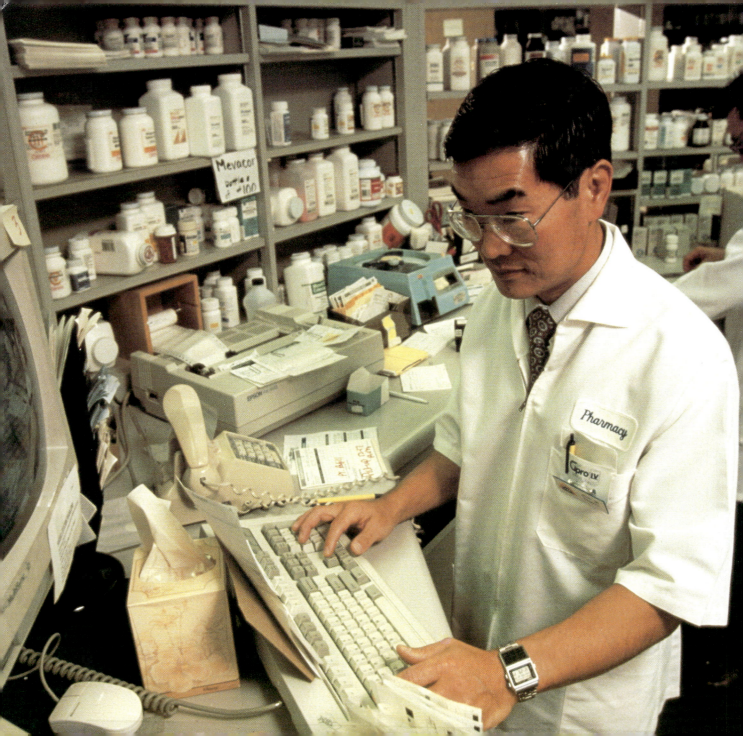

People Who Help Doctors

Nurses help doctors care for sick people. Pharmacists give patients medicine ordered by doctors. Researchers study sicknesses so doctors can cure them.

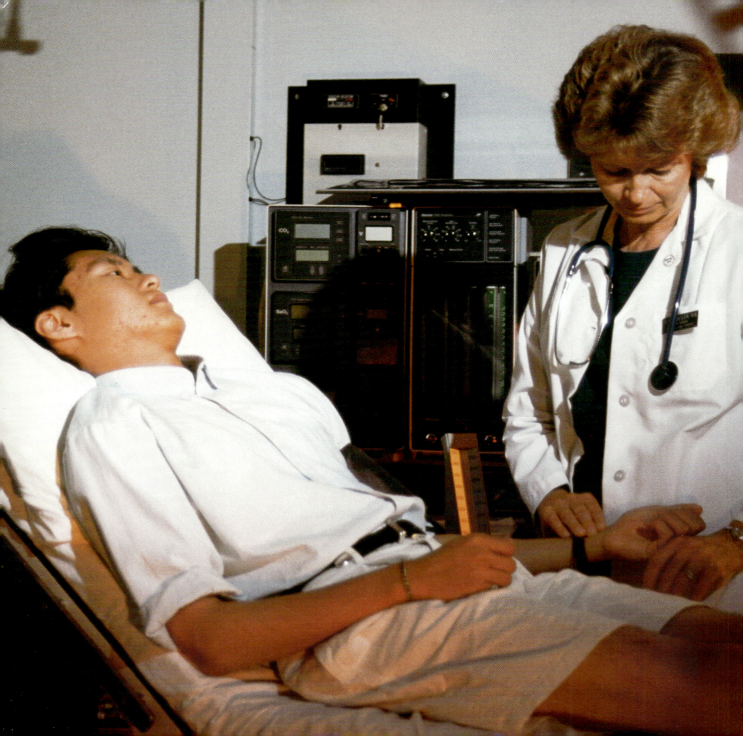

Doctors Help Others

Doctors are important to communities because everyone gets sick. Doctors help people get well and stay well. Doctors help people stay healthy and live a long time.

Hands On: Make Your Own Stethoscope

Doctors use a stethoscope to listen to the sounds in your chest. One of these sounds is your heartbeat. Your heartbeat should be strong and even.

You can use a Styrofoam cup to listen to another person's heartbeat. The cup will be your stethoscope.

1. Cut off the small end of a Styrofoam cup.
2. Place the large end against the other person's chest. Place it in the center or to the left side of the chest.
3. Put your ear to the small end of the cup. Listen very carefully.
4. Check to see if the other person's heart has a regular beat.

Words to Know

checkup (CHEK-uhp)—an examination to see if a person is healthy

community (kuh-MEW-nuh-tee)—a group of people who live in the same area

patient (PAY-shuhnt)—a person who comes to a doctor for a checkup or for medical help

pediatrician (pee-dee-uh-TRI-shuhn)—a doctor who sees only babies and children

pharmacist (FAR-muh-sist)—a trained person who prepares and sells medicine

stethoscope (STETH-uh-skope)—a medical tool used to listen to the sounds in a patient's chest

Read More

Bowman-Kruhm, Mary and Claudine G. Wirths. *A Day in the life of a Doctor.* New York: PowerKids Press, 1997.

Moses, Amy. *Doctors Help People.* Plymouth, Minn.: Child's World, 1997.

Saunders-Smith, Gail. *The Doctor's Office.* Field Trips. Mankato, Minn.: Pebble Books, 1998.

Internet Sites

Going to the Doctor

http://www.aboutchildrenshealth.com/library/weekly/aa071300a.htm

Kids Health

http://KidsHealth.org/kid

Your Gross and Cool Body

http://yucky.kids.discovery.com/noflash/body/index.html

Index